1940s EARLY

fashionable clothing from the sears catalogs

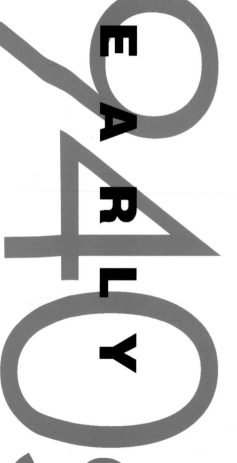

Tina Skinner

Photography by Jenna Palecko Schuck

Schiffer Publishing Ltd

4880 Lower Valley Road, Atglen, PA 19310 USA

Library of Congress Cataloging-in-Publication Data

Skinner, Tina.
Fashionable clothing from the Sears catalogs : early
1940s / Tina Skinner.
p. cm.
ISBN 0-7643-1755-5 (Paperback)
1. Clothing and dress--Catalogs. 2. Costume--Collec-
tors and collecting--United States--History--20th cen-
tury--Catalogs. 3. Rostume--United States--History-
-20th century--Catalogs. 4. Sears, Roebuck and Com-
pany--Catalogs. I. Title.
TT555 .S555 2003
391'.009'044--dc21
2002014197

Designed by Bonnie M. Hensley
Cover design by Bruce M. Waters
Type set in Zurich XCn BT/Zurich BT

ISBN: 0-7643-1755-5
Printed in China
1 2 3 4

Images used in this book are from the Sears Catalogs © Sears, Roebuck and Co.,
and are used with permission.

Fall/Winter 1939 2-5, 13, 14, 19-21, 24, 25, 28, 29, 35, 39, 41, 43-45, 47, 49, 51, 53, 55,
57, 59-61, 65, 68-72, 75, 78, 80, 83, 84, 87, 88, 93, 94, 96, 101, 104, 106, 109, 112,
114, 115, 119, 126, 127, 131, 133, 135, 138, 145, 147, 152, 167, 174, 179, 203, 206,
214, 219, 226, 238, 239, 267, 289, 325, 326, 346, 347, 402, 404, 407, 470

Fall/Winter 1940 3, 4, 7, 8, 14, 35, 44, 45, 56, 63, 65, 69, 71, 88, 91, 92, 94, 97, 102, 104,
107, 109, 110, 113, 116, 137, 161, 178, 191, 196, 213, 214, 249, 291, 293, 294, 302,
306, 309, 318, 350, 355, 371, 381, 383, 385, 386, 392-394, 398, 402, 403, 413, 468,
475

Fall/Winter 1941 15, 19, 33, 35, 37, 51, 53, 56-58, 61, 65, 81, 83, 85, 87, 88, 91, 97, 104,
107, 109, 113, 115, 116, 122, 133, 138, 141-143, 155, 157, 159, 161-163, 215, 231,
233, 245, 279, 295, 305, 311, 315, 324, 330, 376, 396, 404, 405, 416, 418-420, 425,
427-431, 465, 485, 513, 515, 523, 525

Spring/Summer 1941 12-14, 17, 21-24, 28, 29, 31, 33-35, 39, 43, 54, 55, 59, 61, 63, 71,
73, 74, 76, 83, 85-89, 117-120, 150-152, 163, 171, 180, 228, 234, 257-259, 261, 262,
270, 272, 273, 279, 281, 289, 321, 328, 343, 346, 347, 349

Fall/Winter 1942 cover, 5, 7, 9, 12, 15, 17-19, 21, 25, 27, 31, 33, 35, 37, 38, 41, 42, 44, 46,
47, 55, 63-65, 72, 73, 76, 78, 81, 83, 85, 97, 99, 100, 105, 141, 142, 145, 147, 159,
199, 209, 211-213, 220, 258, 260, 265, 288, 289, 301, 323, 328, 332, 335-342, 351-
354, 359, 373, 377-379, 381, 384, 385, 386-388, 393, 395, 399, 401, 402, 464

Published by Schiffer Publishing Ltd.
4880 Lower Valley Road
Atglen, PA 19310
Phone: (610) 593-1777; Fax: (610) 593-2002
E-mail: Schifferbk@aol.com
Please visit our web site catalog at **www.schifferbooks.com**
We are always looking for people to write books on new and related subjects. If you
have an idea for a book please contact us at the above address.

This book may be purchased from the publisher.
Include $3.95 for shipping.
Please try your bookstore first.
You may write for a free catalog.

In Europe, Schiffer books are distributed by
Bushwood Books
6 Marksbury Ave.
Kew Gardens
Surrey TW9 4JF England
Phone: 44 (0) 20 8392-8585; Fax: 44 (0) 20 8392-9876
E-mail: Bushwd@aol.com
Free postage in the U.K., Europe; air mail at cost.

Contents

Introduction

The prices shown reflect the author's personal tastes, as well as fashion trends current at the time of this writing. Though many of these styles recycle on the fashion scene, the garment industry is quick to mass-produce new knock-offs quickly. This forces secondhand and old-stock dealers to remain competitive in pricing, and to search for the most unique items. Likewise, if the garment enjoys fleeting moment of revival on the fashion scene, it can command a premium price.

This book is a visual tour of a wonderful era of American history. Caught up in patriotism, united by common goals and a naïve unity of purpose, these pages document a nation thriving to be thrifty while serving all.

Women, ever the primary audience of Sears fashion catalogs, were donning slacks and work clothes and heading off to factory jobs. Still tempted by beautiful tailored dresses, they were also donning "mannish" suits and "man-tailored" work clothes to "help support him" in the war effort. Styles were overwhelmingly blue, with adjectives like "navy," "cadet," and "soldier." Stripes, plus a splash of red and white, were spread all over the junior and infant styles, and the adults were in on the action, too. Catalog copy unabashedly "saluted" styles that would "win votes" and put wearers in a "military mood."

Not surprisingly, the men's fashion pages were thin in these times, with few able bodies available that weren't already donned in official uniforms. Full-pages in the Sears catalogs urged families to invest in War Bonds, and support the men overseas.

Here is a lovely, lily-white look at what Americans were wearing in the early 1940s. Everyone is thin, even those modeling maternity clothes. The only exceptions are modestly sized women for some of the "Trimline" apparel and a few gray hairs on the "gracious lady" styles.

From the corseted foundation garments to the tightly cinched and narrow fashions, this was an era that demanded conformity. It is also a fabulously elegant time for fashion, when even everyday dresses were fitted and flattering.

Unfortunately, or perhaps fortunately, few in today's climate are willing to sacrifice comfort for this kind of flattery in their everyday wear, and most of the garments that have survived go wanting in thrift shops and resale boutiques. A value guide in brackets is meant as only that – an average value of what dealers and collectors can expect to find on the market, set to fall between the bargains found in charity thrift shops and those garments showcased in trendy resale boutiques. The original prices are also included, generally rounded to the nearest dollar, and the caption text was distilled directly from the catalog copy to provide details about the fabrics, colors, tailoring terminology, and a simple taste for the times.

Because of their age, many of these items are highly collectible, particularly women's shoes, hats, and handbags. With regard to the women's clothing, many of the pastel colors are simply not appealing to today's consumer, though black and navy never go out of style. Denim items are always a hot ticket for resale.

These garments also carry a big advantage in the costume world, as this is undoubtedly the most recreated era in stage and film.

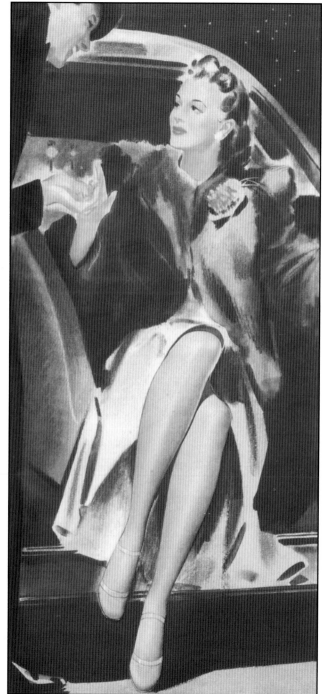

Women's Fashions

Dress Wear

A color-drenched season bursts upon a color-loving people, gay, carefree, and keen for the brighter side of life. [$5-15] Fall/winter 1939-40

Your correct costume can be not only one bright color, but several. No matter your sex or your age, your accessories are gaily hued. [$] Fall/winter 1939-40

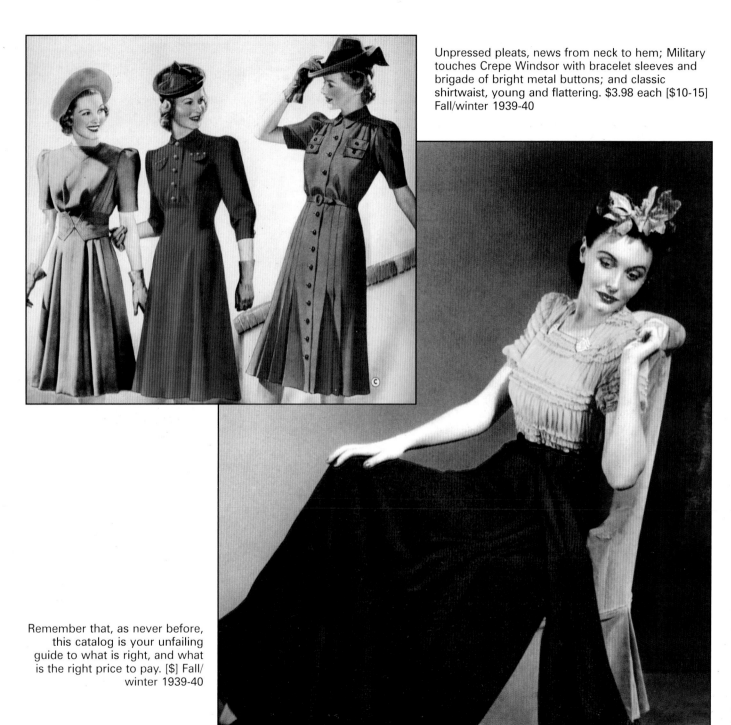

Unpressed pleats, news from neck to hem; Military touches Crepe Windsor with bracelet sleeves and brigade of bright metal buttons; and classic shirtwaist, young and flattering. $3.98 each [$10-15] Fall/winter 1939-40

Remember that, as never before, this catalog is your unfailing guide to what is right, and what is the right price to pay. [$] Fall/winter 1939-40

Put color in your life, sheer rayon chiffon blouse and rayon pebble crepe skirt. $9 [$15-20] Fall/winter 1939-40

Most for your money, rayon dresses: Colorful polka dots, detachable color; Pleated bodice with slim-fitted hips and flaring hemline; Ever-smart shirtwaist dress. $1.98 each. [$5-15] Fall/winter 1939-40

Gracious Lady Fashions: dignified clothes for the older woman: polka dot or plain; prints are always pretty; and flattering soft fullness with a touch of lace. All in navy, black, or nuberry wine. $2-5 [$5-10] Fall/winter 1939-40

Background dresses are beloved by all fashion-wise women. A perfect background dress with its own jewelry can be changed with your own jewelry, flowers, or any other accessories. $2.48 each. [$5-15] Fall/winter 1939-40

Background dresses complete with choice of accessory: bangle bracelet and necklace, corsage, or bolero jacket — what every woman wants. $5-6 [$5-15] Fall/winter 1939-40

Present a new you looking slimmer and younger: nailheads on a new spun rayon that simulates soft, sheer wool; stripe or dot to slenderize with fashion's new notion, long sleeves that are kind to full figures; cartridge pleats and gored skirt; or dyed-to-match cotton lace on rayon crepe dress. $3-4 each [$5-15] Fall/winter 1939-40

Taper off Pounds: two-piece jacket dress, navy with wine trim or black with Skipper blue. $6. Rib weave dress with exquisite scalloping encircling low square panel of the neck and cuffs, in Nuberry wine with Aster pink, navy with Copen blue, black with Skipper Blue, or teal with gold. $5. [$5-15] Fall/winter 1939-40

9

The dress America Adores, the live-in-it jacket dress. $7 [$10-20] Fall/winter 1939-40

Young women's dresses: You'll look your very best in this feminine frock with shirred sleeves, young skirt with un-pressed pleats. $4. Specially proportioned high cowl neckline, accented waistline, and graceful skirt with all-over Schiffli embroi-dery on rayon pebble crepe. $5. This ensemble is practically a fall and winter wardrobe. Bolero jacket is edged with Persian-effect fur fabric, an expensive detail. $8 [$5-20] Fall/winter 1939-40

It's fun to wear a party frock that men and girls admire. Flowers for your dress, your hair in royal blue or white. $3. Bouffant dress with bolero jacket, aqua blue, rose, or black. $7. Fashion sleeves for evening, your glimmering gown's a spotlight in aqua blue and white. $4. [$5-15] Fall/winter 1939-40

Live in a perfect whirl, full skirts that are pleated, gathered, gored. Princess in rayon crepe with loads of gay, contrasting flowers at your throat. $4. Rayon crepe jacket dress with contrasting bodice, navy with Copen blue or black with limegreen. $5. Rustles as you walk taffeta, handsome for dancing, colorful embroidery. $4. [$5-15] Fall/winter 1939-40

Trimline Fashions slenderize by their clever use of color. Bolero effect dress, V-neck bracelet sleeves; Trapunto trim needlework in gold around neckline and sleeves, and allover embroidery. $3.98 each. [$5-15] Fall/winter 1939-40

Be smart – mix your own for evening. Dramatic jacket blouse, gay glitter sweater, and formal-length skirts, $3 each. [$10-25] Fall/winter 1940

For a Glamorous Evening

"Heart Throb" jacket gown of rayon taffeta, white, aqua, or rose, $5. "Spotlight" taffeta gown, white, rose, or light blue, $3. [$5-15] Fall/winter 1940

44D . . SEARS, ROEBUCK AND CO.

Dress-and-jacket costumes ... so smart each outfit equals two, $7 each. [$5-20] Fall/winter 1940

New long line jacket over pleated skirt, with hand-worked scrolls on pockets and collar, dark blue or black, $10. Blouse-back dress with ruffled Pierrot collar, navy, brown, or black, $7. [$10-20] Fall/winter 1940

Keep That Date IN A SHEER!

Lace dress with pin-tucked V-bodice; rayon marquisette with applied flower pattern and embroidered collar; filmy sheer-topped dress, necklace included, and bolero dress with patriotic stripes. $4-7. [$5-15] Spring/summer 1941

The perfect black coat with a separate silver fox scarf, $30. [$35-50] Worn with a dressy frock in the new autumn pastels, $7. [$5-15] Fall/winter 1940

Opposite page, bottom right: For you who are 5 ft. 3 in. or less: perfect fit button front, $4, and sheer yoke, $6. [$5-15] Fall/winter 1940

13

Jacket dresses give you extra value: a wear alone dress plus a wear-with-all jacket: Military mood, three-piece change around, and full-length coat plus dress. $7 each. [$5-15] Spring/summer 1941

All rayon sheer with organdy collar, lace dress with self belt, young two piece, rayon crepe with long waistline, and color contrast dress in browns, blues, or red and white. [$5-15] Spring/summer 1941

Springtime blue enlivened with snowy white: the coat, $13; the suit, $9, and the dress, $7. [$5-15] Spring/summer 1941

Trimline dresses for the gracious lady: coat and dress ensemble, lacy flatterer, and sheer loveliness, $5-7. [$5-15] Spring/summer 1941

Classic tailored shirt frock in Sears' best quality wool flannel, $8. [$5-15] Fall/winter 1941-42

Dresses with radiant young charm: frilled collar on fine rayon crepe, cotton lace flattery on rayon taffeta slip, and full-length coat with dress, $5-6. [$5-15] Spring/summer 1941

The V-neck frock in Sears' best quality rayon crepe, $7. [$5-15] Fall/winter 1941-42

The all-important basic dress: flattering V-neck frock and dickey dress. Good quality, $3; better quality, $5; best quality, $7. [$5-15] Fall/winter 1942-43

The shirtfrock and button-front, two popular Kerrybrooke classics with superb tailoring and styling. Good quality, $4; better quality, $7; and best quality, 9. [$5-15] Fall/winter 1942-43

Sears famous $4.98 dresses, classic fashions
with top quality tailoring in long-wearing fabrics.
[$5-15] Fall/winter 1942-43

Our finest virgin wool dresses: dressmaker style
wool crepe and famous plunging neckline style.
[$5-15] Fall/winter 1942-43

Sears' famous $4.98 dresses: button-front
dickey dress and dress-up shirtfrock. [$5-15]
Fall/winter 1942-43

Best quality rayon fashions: slimming yoke-top dress in aqua or wine, and contrasting tucked panel, black with aqua or navy with soldier blue, $5.98 each. [$5-15] Fall/winter 1942-43

Most wanted styles: smart midriff classic in soldier blue or black and pleated frill shirtfrock in soldier blue or navy, $5.98 each. [$5-15] Fall/winter 1942-43

Ⓐ 12-button Reefer $9.98   Ⓑ 5-button Reefer $9.98   Ⓒ The Boxy Swagger $9.98   Ⓓ Newest Wrap-tie $9.

Ⓔ Velveteen trim $9.98   Ⓕ Reversible Reefer $9.98   Ⓖ Plaid Reversible $9.98   Ⓗ Boxy Reversible $9.

12 . . SEARS, ROEBUCK AND CO. ♡   All these coats described on opposite page. For Hats, see millinery section.

Career

Fashion-right colors, new wool-like textures. $1 each, 2 for $1.95. [$5-10] Fall/winter 1939-40

Work-play clothes: indigo blue overall denim jacket, $2, overalls, $2, and slacks, $1. [$60-75] Shirts and slacks in Indestructo chambray, $1 each. [$35-45] Fall/winter 1939-40

Professional uniforms, now Sanforized: their better fit is permanent. $2-3. [$15-25] Fall/winter 1939-40

Pick a Bargain

... AND PAY THE EASY WAY, IF YOU LIKE ... SEE PAGE 11 $2⁹⁸ EACH

Pick a Bargain: Contrast checked top; bolero-effect dress; slenderizing lines emphasized by stripes with detachable school girl collar; and a dress that spells your name, or nickname, up to five letters you can sew on yourself. $2.98 each. [$5-15] Fall/winter 1939-40

Three smart girls in duo-spun rayon; Henna Rust, Rancho rose, Skipper blue, or Hockey green. $3-5. [$5-15] Fall/winter 1939-40

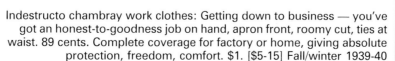

Indestructo chambray work clothes: Getting down to business — you've got an honest-to-goodness job on hand, apron front, roomy cut, ties at waist. 89 cents. Complete coverage for factory or home, giving absolute protection, freedom, comfort. $1. [$5-15] Fall/winter 1939-40

Back-button overalls, high-waist slacks, wool snowcloth pants, and wool flannel "Butcher Boy" jacket. $1-3. [$25-45] Fall/winter 1939-40

THE MORE *Change-Abouts*

Play! Work! Shop! . . . this smart economical way! On these two pages is great variety of colorful Change-Abouts you can shift around to suit your own individual taste. It's easy to have two or three at these very low prices, and easier still with Sears Easy Payment Plan. See Page 11.

TAKE TO LOVELY NEW COLORS
IN THE SEASON'S MOST FLATTERING MATERIALS

$1⁹⁸ Each   Any 2 For $3⁸⁸

America's Newest Fashions: jacket frocks are news; taffetta rustles in again; stripes are so becoming; scallops score a fashion scoop; and if it looks like a bolero it's smart. $2 [$5-15] Fall/winter 1939-40

Yes, you can wear the new silhouette, dashing, you, gay with nipped waistline, broad shoulders, swirling hem — flattering as orchids from your husband, navy, henna, or burgundy. $8 [$10-20] Fall/winter 1939-40

"Silhouette"—The suit that looks like a dress—brief unlined jacket, dramatically full skirt, myriad stitched pleats—all as new as this minute. Beautifully tailored in the famous Juilliard All Wool Crepe, our very best quality. Misses' Sizes: 12, 14, 16, 18, 20 only. State size and color; see Size Scale on Page 37. Shpg. wt., 1 lb. 10 oz.
17 D 5830—Navy Blue, Henna Rust 643, Burgundy Wine 514............$7.98

Clever coveralls, work shirt and pants, and jacket and slick slacks in a variety of fabrics and colors, including cotton, rayon, and wool blends, gabardine, twill, and woven stripe suiting. Including navy, rust, light gray, aquamarine, green, and coral. [$15-25] Fall/winter 1940

Three colors that sing a song of burnished autumn shades in a two-piece jacket dress. $5. [$5-15] Fall/winter 1939-40

Indestructo work clothes of the same Sanforized chambray material used for men's heavy duty work shirts. [$15-30] Fall/winter 1940

Miss America: the perfect all-purpose uniform in cotton poplin or rayon sharkskin, $1-3. [$5-15] Fall/winter 1940

From Kentucky, a coat of enduring fashion, $16, and a classic shirtfrock of wool flannel, $8. [$5-15] Fall/winter 1940

Cubana Cloth

A SENSATIONAL SUCCESS FABRIC

4-STAR FEATURE
with four great
value points:

* New Rayon fabric, usually found in dresses twice Sears prices
* Has crisp, porous texture; linen-like finish; defies wrinkles
* Clear rich colors are equally hand-some in print or plain; in light shades or dark
* Tested washfast; safe in LUX

Two-piece dress with dots, print or plain one-piece casual dress, dress plus jacket, and striped or plain side-button dress, $3-4. [$5-15] Spring/summer 1941

Treat yourself to tawny browns, heavenly blues, rose, and mossy green: two colors make this one-piece dress twice as smart; stunning dress with pert peplum, narrow self ruffles; three-piece sensation with big buttons to hold gored skirt and blouse together, and an elegant costume of chiffon coat over rayon crepe with ruffle shirred pockets. [$] Spring/summer 1941

A	B	C
2 Shades or 2 colors combine in soft harmony	All One Color new flattering silhouette	Flash of White against dark skirt and bolero
$2.98	$3.98	$4.98

Twin Print coat and dress... extra value

NEW
Man-Tailored Suits

A MATCH FOR THE MEN

with longer jackets and lighter padding; slimmer sleeves. Center-pleat skirt.

Fully man-tailored from neck to hem!

1. Collars felled and shrunk to fit
2. Shoulders squared, smartly padded
3. The lapels are skillfully interlined with good Menswear Canvas
4. Jacket fronts well interlined with Menswear Canvas to maintain shape
5. Well-made pockets will not sag
6. All buttonholes resist fraying
7. Armholes reinforced for longer wear

Man-Copied Sack Suit in Choice of Fabrics   Classic Link Button Suit—in 3 Classic Fabrics

Perfected Fit Dresses..Save Alteration

Sizes 16½ to 26½ fit, and flatter, women 5 feet, 3 in. . . . or shorter. Belts never too wide; necks are becoming; and gored skirts add to your youth and height

Woven stripe or plain in Cadet blue, rose, or clay brown grounds, flower-patterned lace in beige, navy, rose, or powder blue; coat and dress ensemble in navy or black over colorful print, and jacket dress ensemble in navy, rose, teal, aqua, and brown. $4-6. [$5-15] Spring/summer 1941

Man-copied sack suit in choice of wool/cotton blend, wool suede, or wool worsted gabardine, tan, brown, or navy. $8-13. Classic link button [$] Spring/summer 1941

Perfected Fit Dresses..Save Alteration

Sizes 16½ to 26½ fit, and flatter, women 5 feet, 3 in. . . . or shorter. Belts never too wide; necks are becoming; and gored skirts add to your youth and height

Woven-stripe on blue, rose, or brown or plain spun rayon in blue, rose, or beige, $3; flower-patterned lace with rayon taffeta, $4; coat and dress ensemble, $5; and jacket and dress ensemble in plain Celanese rayon or printed rayon, $4 or 6. [$5-15] Spring/summer 1941

TRIMLINE SUCCESS DRESSES

104 .. SEARS, ROEBUCK AND CO.

Trimline success dresses for stout women, sizes 39-53, $5-8. [$5-15] Fall/winter 1941-42

LOOK FOR THESE $10.98 WORKMANSHIP FEATURES
- Youthfully Cut, Gored Skirts
- Quality Self-material Buttons
- Crown Zip Side-Seam Plackets
- Taped Hems and Pinked Seams
- White Collar that BUTTONS On

The newer, smarter dresses add a jacket, for double duty in charm, style, and economy, $7. [$5-20] Fall/winter 1941-42

Warm, sheer wools with 10 rabbit hair added: Charmode scroll-pocket frock and button-front dress, $9. [$10-20] Fall/winter 1941-42

Our finest dresses in wool: button-front style, insertions of pleating, and fly-front frock, $9 each. [$5-15] Fall/winter 1941-42

Rayon frocks: dress-up frock with plaster-white buttons and shirtwaist dress with convertible collar, $5 each. [$5-15] Fall/winter 1941-42

Charmode **Dresses for a Gracious Lady**

Dresses for a gracious lady: rayon in plain or dotted navy or black, $2; printed or plain rayon in navy or black, $3; shirtwaist frock in navy, black, or gray, $6; and success style with convertible neckline and adjustable hem in navy or black, $5. [$5-15] Fall/winter 1941-42

Best cotton dress values: $2.79 each. [$5-15] Fall/winter 1942-43

Super-wear work clothes, comfort cut, in blue cotton, $1-2. [$25-50] Fall/winter 1941-42

Fine features add good looks and greater values to these cotton dresses, $2.79 each. [$5-15] Fall/winter 1942-43

For factory, for farm and home: heavy duty denim, work cloth, and corduroy, $1.49-$3. [$25-45] Fall/winter 1942-43

Sturdy comfortable clothes, cotton work cloth and corduroy, $2-4. [$25-45] Fall/winter 1942-43

Sturdy, comfortable clothes . . .

Sears famous $4.98 dresses: softer button-front and saddle-stitched shirtfrock. [$5-15] Fall/winter 1942-43

Our greatest suit values: the seven-button suit, classic cardigan suit, and classic three-button suit, $15 each. [$25-35] Fall/winter 1942-43

Glen Plaid

Herringbone

Kerrybrooke
CLASSIC

*Kerrybrooke is Sears own name for
casual clothes . . Styles of the minute . . fashions wearable for years.

Pin-Stripe   ♡ PAGE 27 SUITS

Collar
closed

Popular-priced classic styles: menswear gray flannel, button-up suit, and casual version of link-button suit,
$14 each. [$] Fall/winter 1942-43

Link-button classic suit, man-tailored to give lasting wear, fit,
style, $13-17. [$25-35] Fall/winter 1942-43

Sportswear and Casual

Sing a Song of Color with copies of high priced fashions. Only Sears has them in cottons. The little jacket dress all America is wild about, two-piece plaid-and-plain; pris cables hummed with the news of the shirtwaist dress, with cardigan neck and contrasting skirt; America's gone Plaid Mad hew with velveteen collar and buttons and the look and feel of wool; or play the Gypsy with exciting shirtwaist and skirt made into one. $1 each. [$5-15] Fall/winter 1939-40

It's the American way . . . to live in a dress with a jacket. $6. Scotty cap, $1. [$5-20] Fall/winter 1939-40

Two smart dresses, sizes to 57. $1. [$5-15] Fall/winter 1939-40

Change-abouts: Colorful skirts, blouses, sweaters, jackets – the casual put-together clothes America loves best. [$5-15] Fall/winter 1939-40

Change-abouts... THE CLOTHES

Colorful skirts, blouses, sweaters, jackets—the casual "put-together" clothes America loves best! Sears do them in the best American tradition, for casuals must be young, spirited, right for any age or place.

Ⓐ **New Windbreaker Style.** Just about the youngest blouse you could own! Soft dull All Spun Rayon in a Scarlet, Bright Blue, or White—to complement the many jackets and skirts you'll wear it with. Young collarless neckline, wide snug waistband, shirred yoke, novelty wooden buttons that fasten up front.
$1.00
Colors: Scarlet, Bright Blue 217, or White. Bust Sizes: 30, 32, 34, 36, 38, 40 in. State size and color.
77 D 2965—Shipping weight, 7 oz.......$1.00

Ⓑ **Plaid or Plain Skirt.** Wherever you go, this is the most popular skirt in America! Gayly pleated all around, with the pleats stitched-down flat over hips, swinging out gracefully when you walk. Crown zip placket, two-button waistband closing. One of Sears smart ways of saving.
$3.59
Waist Sizes: 24, 26, 28, 30, 32, 34 in. State size, color. Size Scale Page 90. Shipping weight, each, 1 pound.
Finest Quality All Wool Plaid
7 D 2916—Red, Black and Gray Plaid; or Bright-Blue, Black and Gray Plaid....$3.59
Fine Quality Plain All Wool Crepe
7 D 2530—Lt. Navy, Black, Strawberry Rose 515.....$2.98
Fine All Spun Rayon Ribbed Weave
7 D 2531—Pigeon Gray 805 or Navy....$1.98

Ⓒ **Gadabout Jacket**—smart for town or country, from morning to night... supremely good-looking, delightfully easy to wear. Made of fine quality All Wool Tweed in handsome wide stripes of blending colors spattered with bright contrasting nubs—a tweed you can wear with a wide variety of skirts, sweaters and dresses. Expertly man tailored in new cardigan style, trimly buttoned with square padded shoulders, a stitched seam down the back, sturdy rayon lining.
$4.98
Bust Sizes: 30, 32, 34, 36, 38, 40 in. Length, about 22 in. State size. Shpg. wt., 1 lb. 6 oz.
17 D 2296—Green with colorful Nubs and Stripes
17 D 2297—Brown with colorful Nubs and Stripes.............$4.98

Ⓓ **Newest 4-Gore Flare Skirt** in fine quality All Wool Flannel, dyed in colors to match the sweater pictured below and to blend with jacket described above. One of those simple, well bred four-gore flared skirts that couples beautifully with dressy or sports blouses, sweaters, jackets. Smooth Crown zip hip placket.
$1.98
Waist Sizes: 24, 26, 28, 30, 32, 34 inch. State size; see Size Scale on Page 90. Shipping weight, 12 ounces.
7 D 2933M—Laurel Green
7 D 2934M—Brown 613.............$1.98

Send your order to Sears nearest Mail Order House and allow postage from there. Garments on these two pages selling at $1.98 or over, and catalog number 7 D 3033M sent direct from our New York Fashion Headquarters. All others sent from Sears Mail Order House nearest you.

Numbers after color names refer to Color Graph preceding first index page in back of book.

Ⓔ **Brushed All Wool Zephyr Sweater** →
Click... the busiest little sweater in the world! Soft, fluffy brushed All Wool Zephyr for wear with any casual skirts, slacks, shorts. Youthful boat neck, hug-me-tight waistband. Colors dyed to match skirts 7 D 2933M and 7 D 2934M described above, also in contrasting colors.
$1.00
Colors: Laurel Green, Brown 613, Nude, or White. Bust Sizes: 30, 32, 34, 36, 38, 40 in. State size, color.
7 D 3033 M—Shipping

SOFT GENUINE SUEDE LEATHER

Soft, genuine suede leather, brown, blue, rust, and dark green. $4.50-7. [$75-100] Fall/winter 1939-40

COLORFUL TWO-PIECE SUITS

WATER-REPELLENT . . . FOR WORK, FOR PLAY

Jacket is Sheepskin or Kasha Lined

Colorful two-piece suits for work, for play. Wool snow suits. $8-9. [$30-50] Fall/winter 1939-40

Gay change-abouts for the outdoor scene; ski and snow suits of wool, worsted gabardine, and sanforized cotton poplin. [$5-25] Fall/winter 1939-40

Pegless jodhpurs .. saddle pants for general outdoor wear, hiking, ranch life, vacation, $2-3. [$15-25] Fall/winter 1940

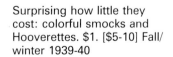

Surprising how little they cost: colorful smocks and Hooverettes. $1. [$5-10] Fall/winter 1939-40

Jodhpurs, breeches, and man-tailored shirts, $1-3. [$5-25]
Fall/winter 1940

Pretty percales, $1. [$5-15]
Fall/winter 1940

Quality coat frocks, $1.39 each.
[$5-15] Fall/winter 1940

Change-arounds to contrast or match: "Little Boy" boxy jacket, $4; dyed-to-match sweater and skirt, $2 each; 2-piece charmer sports shirt and Dutch skirt, $5, shirtwaist outfit in choice of fabrics, $2-4. [$5-15] Fall/winter 1940

Easy-on maternity dresses are the prettiest and most practical ever. [$5-15] Fall/winter 1940

Amazing at This Low Price!
New Fashions in Rayon
Styled like high priced dresses that are New York favorites
See easy terms, inside back cover

$298 Each

New giant plaid in bright scarlet, green, or blue; go-everywhere dress with smocking; pastel appliqué two-piece dress; hood dress with bright embroidery, and bolero effect rayon pebble crepe print, $3 each [$5-15] Fall/winter 1940

Finest novelty cottons in attractive prints, unusual textures: navy or black trimline in stout women's sizes; eyelet pique with button front; dotted cotton voile, and poplin or muslin twin print. [$5-15] Spring/summer 1941

Slenderizing shirtwaist style in striped pique or seersucker; flattering princess lines on flower print; button-front dress with shutter pleats, full-skirted shirtwaist, button-front pique with eyelet trim, and just for juniors printed frock. [$5-15] Spring/summer 1941

Play clothes you'll live in: gay pinafore shirt and shorts; culotte and shirt separates, cotton seersucker three-piece playsuit, and the three-way jerkin set, $1-4. [$5-15] Spring/summer 1941

Spring-and-Summer EXTRAS YOU'LL NEED

Culotte dress, two-piece outfit, slacks suit, overall, and jacket, in navy, green, teal, and blue. [$] Spring/summer 1941

THE NEW SEA-HO

Miss America

SWIM SUIT
With
Up-Lift Brassiere
That Snaps In!

Also Has Separate
Girdle Panties

$2.98

Two-piece beach hit in royal or navy blue, ballerina beauty in sky or royal blue, and two-piece midriff style in red and white or blue and white, $2-3. [$35-45] Spring/summer 1941

Finest-fitting rayon satin suit we've ever sold, black and aqua or royal blue, $3. [$30-40] Spring/summer 1941

Slack suits in California-style or classic style, $3-5. [$5-15] Spring/summer 1941

Washfast cottons in misses', women's, and juniors' sizes, $1 each. [$5-16] Fall/winter 1941-42

Guaranteed cottons, finest quality 80-sq. percales, $1.49. [$5-15] Fall/winter 1941-42

Cavalry twill, they wear so ruggedly, $3.29. [$10-20] Fall/winter 1941-42

$109
EACH
Similar Quality Elsewhere is . . . $139

Searspride HOME FROCKS

Better Quality Washfast 68x72 Percales...Misses, Womens, Juniors Sizes
Zip or Button-ups...Full Cut to Fit...Quality Details...All Seams Pinked

Searspride. [$5-15] Fall/winter 1941-42

All-purpose snow pants and winter-weight sports slacks, all-wool gabardine or snowcloth of reprocessed wool lined with cotton, $4.50-$7. Perfect sports shirt of rayon/wool, $3. Buffalo check shirt of wool/rayon, $3. [$5-15] Fall/winter 1941-42

Sears' best action-cut tapered trouser suit, blue or bright red, $19. All purpose outdoor suits for sports, cold weather, or wear anywhere, $10-14. [$10-20] Fall/winter 1942-43

Your favorite Joan Bradley classic sweaters: the most popular sweater styles you'll find in America today, $2.50. [$10-20] Fall/winter 1942-43

Slacks to work in, play in, live in: $2-4. [$5-15] Fall/winter 1942-43

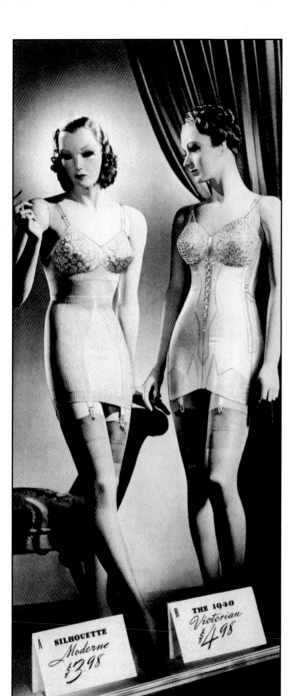

Corset you beautifully in newest nude color. [$5-10] Fall/winter 1939-40

America's favorite classic Joan Bradley sweaters, virgin wool, $2-$2.55. [$10-20] Fall/winter 1942-43

Velvety pin-wale corduroy classics, $3-6. [$10-20] Fall/winter 1942-43

All wool V-neck and convertible collar sweaters, $3.50. [$15-25] Fall/winter 1942-43

Slimmer styles for the shorter woman, and dresses for a gracious lady, $3-6.
[$5-15] Fall/winter 1942-43

Washable Searspride classic
coatdress and V-neck dress, $2-3.
[$5-15] Fall/winter 1942-43

Famous Storkette suit in two-piece slack set, two-piece maternity dress, and slim, dressy effect, $3-5.50 each. [$5-15] Fall/winter 1942-43

Smocked maternity dress in rayon crepe, rayon/cotton blend, or sturdy percale, $2-$4.50 [$5-15] Fall/winter 1942-43

Lingerie

An entire new line of Flatter-ees: foundation wear of combed cotton, cotton/rayon blend, and cotton with 10% wool/2-1/2% silk. 16-25 cents. [$5-15] Fall/winter 1939-40

Do you want relief from that "tired, worn-out feeling?" You should wear a Gale Health Belt. All in one, side lace style, belted foundation, and two-lace health belt. $3-5. [$5-10] Fall/winter 1939-40

Two Lengths for All Height Figures

Two Lengths for All Height Figures

Gale   *Gale*   *Gale*

Two-way stretch lace Lastex tops give free action, 89¢. [$2-5] Fall/winter 1939-40

The most beautiful stockings in all the world, sheer yet, weight for weight the longest wearing, 98¢. [$2-5] Fall/winter 1939-40

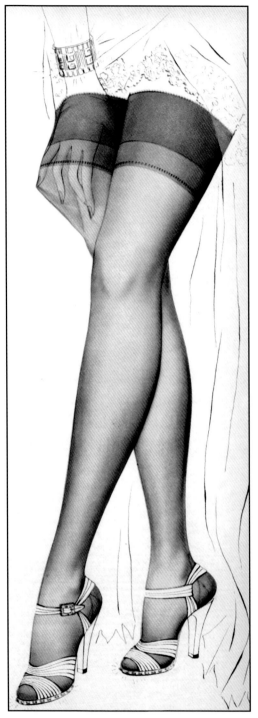

Sears inner belt foundations. [5-15$] Fall/winter 1939-40

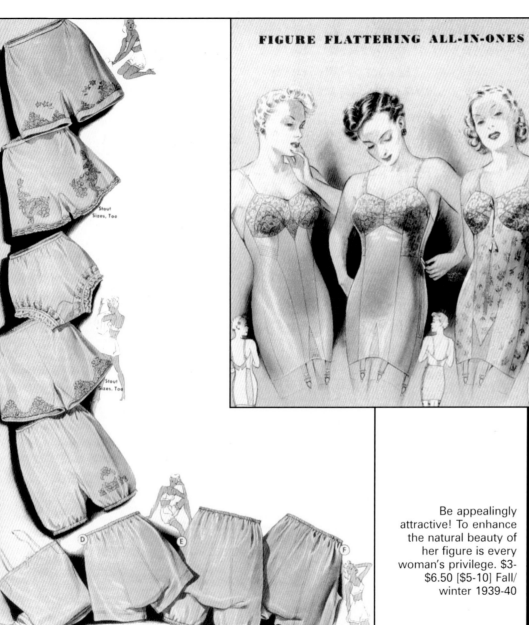

FIGURE FLATTERING ALL-IN-ONES

Figure flattering all-in-ones, $2-3. [$5-10] Fall/winter 1939-40

Double Panel Back
GOOD QUALITY KNIT RAYONS

Loveliness begins with sleek, rayon underwear, flesh and tearose colors, 27¢ to 39¢. [$2-5] Fall/winter 1939-40

Be appealingly attractive! To enhance the natural beauty of her figure is every woman's privilege. $3-$6.50 [$5-10] Fall/winter 1939-40

For fuller figures, enjoy the comfort of firm, two-way stretch, $1.39-$1.94. [$5-15] Spring/summer 1941

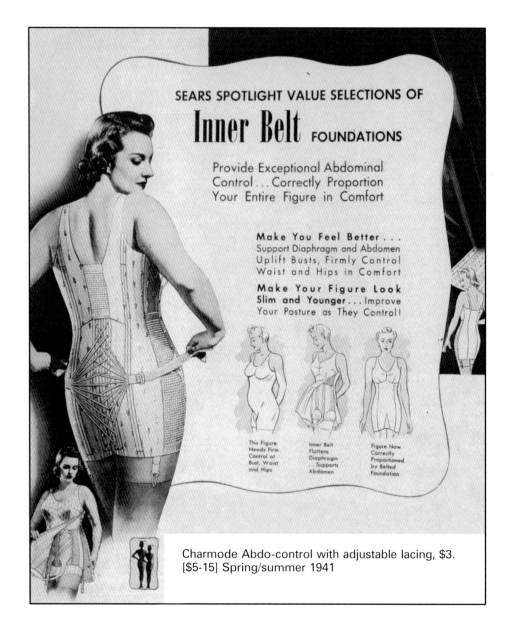

SEARS SPOTLIGHT VALUE SELECTIONS OF

Inner Belt FOUNDATIONS

Provide Exceptional Abdominal Control... Correctly Proportion Your Entire Figure in Comfort

Make You Feel Better... Support Diaphragm and Abdomen Uplift Busts, Firmly Control Waist and Hips in Comfort

Make Your Figure Look Slim and Younger... Improve Your Posture as They Control!

This Figure Needs Firm Control at Bust, Waist and Hips

Inner Belt Flattens Diaphragm ...Supports Abdomen

Figure Now Correctly Proportioned by Belted Foundation

Charmode Abdo-control with adjustable lacing, $3. [$5-15] Spring/summer 1941

Lacy camisole, embroidery trimmed, and famous Perfec-Fit Slip, $1.50-2 [$5-10] Spring/summer 1941

Also Half Sizes for Smaller, Shorter Women

Fine-fitting Francines , priced for savings, $1.29. [$5-10] Fall/winter 1942-43

51

GREAT *Hullabaloo*

All Robes Described on Opposite Page

D Spun Rayon $3.29

C Rayon Taffeta $5.98

B Cotton Chenille $4.49

A Cotton Chenille $2.98

E Rayon Taffeta $4.65

F Rayon Taffeta $2.98
Slub Cotton $1.98

G Rayon French-type Crepe $3.98

206 ◊

House Coats: Heart catchers every one. $3-5. [$5-15; $70-90 for chenille] Fall/winter 1939-40

You Can Buy Pajamas on Easy Terms See Page 11

A
B
C
D

Flannelette Pajamas: June-in-December flower print; style hit "lumberjack" blouse; wide blazer stripes, and favorite Russian-blouse style. $1. [$5-15] Fall/winter 1939-40

Relax, Be Warm and Pretty

Sweeping lines . . . Candlewicks, Chenilles, Corduroys, Rayon Taffetas. Glowing colors.

Cotton Chenille
$2.98
(E)

Cotton Chenille
Misses' Sizes
$3.98
Women's Sizes
$4.48
(D)

Cotton Candlewick
Warm, Washfast Thickly Tufted in Exclusive Designs

(G) $2.98

(H) $3.98

(L) Quilted Rayon Taffeta Print
$5.98
Quilted Plain Rayon Satin
$4.98

Quilted Rayon Taffeta Bed Jacket
$2.98
(M)

(K) Corduroy With Hood
$3.98
Without Hood
$2.98

(F) Slippers 79¢
—Cotton Chenille to match robes (E) and (D) above —order with robes . . . not sold separately.

(J) Celanese Rayon Taffeta
$3.98
Cotton Seersucker
$2.98
Cotton Poplin
$1.98

Garments on these two pages shipped from our Fashion Headquarters in New York City. Send your order to nearest Mail Order House or, for these garments alone, you may send order directly to New York. You pay postage only from nearest Mail Order House. Color numbers refer to Color-Graph in How to Order section at back of book.

Be warm and pretty in flannel housecoats and chenille. [$5-15, $70-90 for chenille] Fall/winter 1940

Lustrous rayon satin or fine cotton jamarettes, $1-2. [$5-15] Fall/winter 1940

Housecoats to make you charming: candy striped, red or blue with white; gleaming white rayon sharkskin, flattery for all sizes in navy or wine print, $1-3. [$5-15] Spring/summer 1941

Housecoat hit, rose or blue on white, $2. [$5-15] Spring/summer 1941

Charmode
HOUSECOAT HITS!

Charmode

Housecoat hits in splashy floral cottons and rayon taffeta, $2.29; cotton candlewicks, $4-5. [$5-15; 70-90 for chenille] Fall/winter 1941-42

Sailorette polka-dot, butcher boy, and gown ensemble, $1.39-4. [$5-15] Fall/winter 1941-42

Luxurious, flattering, and comfortable robes, $4-6. [$5-15; 70-90 for chenille] Fall/winter 1941-42

Charmode **FASHION-FAMOUS ROBES**

Downy and soft, warm as toast. [$5-15] Fall/winter 1941-42

Best quality slumber queens, 98¢. [$5-15] Fall/winter 1941-42

The finest flannelette pajamas you can buy, $1.29. [$5-15] Fall/winter 1941-42

Women's House and Bedroom Slippers

Moccasin-like construction...one-piece felt upper and midsole that holds shape better, gives extra comfort—and longer wear smooth felt insole.

Women's house and bedroom slippers, $1.29 each. [$5-15] Fall/winter 1942-43

Famous Jamarettes in extra heavy flannelette, $2. [$5-15] Fall/winter 1942-43

Our finest flannelettes, pajamas and military housecoat, $2 each. [$5-15] Fall/winter 1942-43

Warm quilted housecoats in lovely flowered prints, $4-7. [$5-15] Fall/winter 1942-43

for beauty, comfort

Charmode·Housecoats for easy hours
Sizes 12 to 20, 38 to 46, 45 to 53

Charmode
HOUSECOATS

Popular styles ... durable, warm

Sizes for Misses (also fit Juniors), Women, Stout Women
Carefully tailored and finished for good fit, long wear.

Best-liked housecoat in seersucker, poplin, and percale, $2-4. Beacon blanket cloth robe, popular short-length, and rayon twill robes, $3-$5.50. [$5-15, $25-50 for seersucker and Beacon blanket] Fall/winter 1942-43

Outerwear

Wonderful, whirling hemlines give you your heart's desire: Princess-fitted muff coat with mink-dyed marmot fur, $18. Persian cloth bolero on an all-wool coat, $12. All wool coat with detachable fur collar, $11. [$20-35] Fall/winter 1939-40

Handsome scrolls of matching embroidery on collar and sleeves of slim-line swagger coat, $15. Tucks, tucks, tucks … back and front, $14. Alternating boucle stripes in dashing 9-gore swing coat with smartly defined waistline, $11. [$20-30] Fall/winter 1939-40

Send for your free copy of our special Fur Fashion Catalog—and remember you can buy on Sears Easy Payment Plan—see Page 11.

Persian effect wool and rayon: have the glorious feeling of owning a fur coat without paying the price, $14. Wool rayon coat with Persian-effect collar, $9. [$30-40] Fall/winter 1939-40

Fabric coats are fashion copies of real Persian fur. Ombre or black with swing silhouette, roll collar, $7. Popular "chunky" new jacket, black, $9. [$15-30] Fall/winter 1939-40

Warmest of all, double-thick all-wool fabrics: Gay young swagger or emphasis on pockets, $15 each. [$15-25] Fall/winter 1939-40

Diagonal weave in a square-shoulder swagger. Wide revers with stunning trapunto stitching. Young swing silhouette with narrow waist, broad shoulders. $8 each. [$15-25] Fall/winter 1939-40

Wonder Value

HI-COLOR.. LONG LIFE.. ALL WOOL FLEECE

$7.98 Each

INCLUDE YOUR NEW COAT IN AN EASY PAYMENT ORDER. See Page II.

SILHOUETTE?

Swirling Hemlines · · · **Unpressed Pleats** · · · **Gores and Flares**

Basque-effect waist and swirling skirt for grace, wool/rayon/cotton, $18. Unpressed pleats for graceful front fullness, $11. Rippled shawl collar of Manchurian dog fur, boucle fabric, $17. [$20-35] Fall/winter 1939-40

FOR EASY PAYMENT PLAN, SEE PAGE 11.

Send your order to Sears nearest Mail Order House and allow postage for that distance. Garments on these two pages will be sent from New York, America's fashion center.

Tweeds that whisper...
Tweeds that shout...
Smart for travel
Or knock-about.

Right for sports,
country, city,
Church or tearoom,
School committee.

Warm and sturdy,
Rain or shine...
Tweeds are perfect,
ANYTIME!

Tweeds . . .

All-wool ombre-striped tweed, $11. New weave wool with double-breasted front, $11. Three-piece wardrobe suit with wolf fur, satin lining, $30. [$15-55] Fall/winter 1939-40

The new tweeds meet the needs of American living: blended plaid in fall tones, $13. Raccoon fur collar on wool/rayon, $18. All wool straight-line silhouette, $10. [$20-30] Fall/winter 1939-40

Luxurious seal-dyed or beaver-dyed buck coney, $35 ($4 down … $5 a month). [$25-50] Fall/winter 1939-40

Glorious values, Gorgeous tweeds: patch-pocket swagger, velveteen trim, or removable zip vestee, $10. [$5-15] Fall/winter 1940

Sports coat winners: 1941's most popular plaid reefer with belted back; wear-with-all coat, and tweed beauty, $8. [$5-15] Spring/summer 1941

Mannish fashion at its best, swashbuckle sports coats, $10. [$5-15] Spring/summer 1941

The ensemble, wear coat or dress separately any hour of the day, $11. [$5-15] Spring/summer 1941

Dressy coats in tailored styles, navy, black, and healther, $10-13. [$5-15] Spring/summer 1941

Wear your coat the new way ... thrown over your shoulders. [$10-20] Fall/winter 1941-42

Fur fashions that last: sable- or bolack-dyed opossum, 24-inch blue fox-dyed guanaco fur, new 32-inch sable-dyed coney fur, and 26-inch black-dyed Manchurian dog. [$50-75] Fall/winter 1941-42

Wool herringbone tweeds are America's No. 1 favorite for coats, $11-20. [$5-15] Fall/winter 1941-42

Treat yourself to a bargain value, plus best-selling style: new idea sagger coat, double-breasted reefer, and record breaker success – we began to get fan-mail from happy wearers, $8 each. [$5-15] Fall/winter 1941-42

Well-tailored all-wool coats, $10. [$5-15] Fall/winter 1941-42

Topcoat-rained coats, lined or unlined styles:
$4-8. [$5-15] Fall/winter 1941-42

Left: All-wool tweed coats for extra long wear:
reefer, leather-button balmacaan, and wrap-tie,
$13 each. [$5-15] Fall/winter 1942-43

Right: Shaded ombre plaid coats in boxy,
double-breasted reefer, and wrap-tie styles, $15
each. [$5-15] Fall/winter 1942-43

PAGE 15

PAGE 17

Big fluffy fur collars on thick warm coats, $27. [$10-20] Fall/winter 1942-43

At left, back view of Balmacaan coat

At right, back view of wrap-tie coat

Balmacaan $27.50   Wrap-tie $27.50

Kerrybrooke is our own name for casual clothes ... styles of the minute ... fashions wearable for years.

▽ PAGE 7 . . . . COATS

Kerrybrooke
POLO COATS

Our greatest coat values: classic balmacaan and double-breasted wrap-tie coat, both in warm wool/camel hair/mohair fleece, $27.50. [$30-40] Fall/winter 1942-43

Finest coats, best furs, best wool fabrics: fully gored back, tie-belt and dressmaker coat, both in black. [$30-50] Fall/winter 1942-43

Classic reefer and classic boy coat in herringbone tweed wool, $27.50. [$10-20] Fall/winter 1942-43

Trimline coat: gored reefer, boxy coat with built-up neckline, and dress coat, $15-20. [$5-20] Fall/winter 1942-43

The Reefer and the Boxy Coat: most popular coats in America, $13-30. [$5-20] Fall/winter 1942-43

Leather jackets: fitted princess style in suede or smooth leather, $10. [$40-55] Fall/winter 1942-43

Teddy bear wool shortie and Trooper Coat with Alpaca wool lining, $15-6 each. [$40-55] Fall/winter 1942-43

Cardigan jacket in smart 26-inch length: black jackal wolf, opossum, dyed skunk-stripes, $40-70. [$60-75] Fall/winter 1942-43

Cooney fur coat, dyed to resemble seal or beaver, $75. [$60-75] Fall/winter 1942-43

Shoes, Hats, and Accessories

Black suede, utterly devastating accent for autumn femininity, $3. [$30-40] Fall/winter 1939-40

Wintergreen

American Beauty

Combine three shades in a single dress, or echo it again and again in your costume, as shown in the color tableaux. Outstanding accents of the season are Sears Wintergreen, and American Beauty. Fall/winter 1939-40

Color, color, everywhere: in black, wine, teal, navy, green, Bittersweet, Wintergreen, and American Beauty. [$30-40] Fall/winter 1939-40

Velvet brings out the sparkle in your eyes: bumper-brim hat, turban, and grosgrain little-girl streamers, $1-2. [$20-30] Fall/winter 1939-40

Simulated leather and suede bags, 59 cents. [$30-40] Fall/winter 1939-40

Lacey neckwear, quilted bolero jacket, and removable 3-initialed pin. [$2-5] Fall/winter 1939-40

For that little girl look, bright toppers make quick color changes. [$2-5] Fall/winter 1939-40

Up-rolled, easy to wear hats, $1-2. [$15-25] Fall/winter 1939-40

Glowing shades in a hat designed by a woman who makes hats for royalty, movie stars, and millionaire-esses! $3. This is your year to dress like a wren, wear lively plaid, $2. Hand-draped, two-tone hat, $2. [$15-25] Fall/winter 1939-40

Our finest hiking boot, $3-5.50. [$50-75] Fall/winter 1939-40

BLACK OR BROWN

FOR THE OUT-OF-DOORS LOVER · · THE RANCH WOMAN OR HIKER

HERE IS PROTECTION, STAMINA, GOOD LOOKS, LOW PRICE!

Pleats

FOR THE TRUE FEMINIST

® Swanky Tie with pleated inserts
$3.29 PR.

Ⓨ Angelic step-in with pleated winged front
$3.29 PR.

Pleated skirts that swing in the breeze—pleated frills to flatter fresh young faces—and, fashion-wise women tripping gaily along in pleated shoes, the most delightfully whimsical fancy of the present season.

Ⓝ Pump with pleats on vamp. High or Cuban heel
$2.98 PR.

Alligator ···THE PERENNIAL PET

Ⓥ Trim, sportive alligator pump
$1.89 PR.

Ⓟ Square toe, walled last tie
$1.79 PR.

Ⓜ New oval cut-outs on alligator tie
$1.95 PR.

Send your order to Sears nearest Mail Order House and allow postage from there. All items marked with triangle ▲ sent from Chicago or Philadelphia

For the true feminist, flagrant flattery. [$30-40] Fall/winter 1939-40

Shock absorbing, nurses' type walking oxford. [$10-20] Fall/winter 1939-40

BLACK KID
SMOOTH WHITE
BLACK SUEDE

Ventilated Airflow

NURSES' TYPE OXFORD

CHOICE OF
BLACK SUEDE
BLACK KID
WHITE KID

$3.85 PAIR

New ways to look young. $1- 1.70. [$15-25] Fall/winter 1939-40

Deep-fitting felt and side-roll brim, black, rust, navy, green, brown, or wine, $1.69 each. [$15-25] Fall/winter 1940

Beautifully matched accessories in the newest colors. [$10-25] Fall/winter 1940

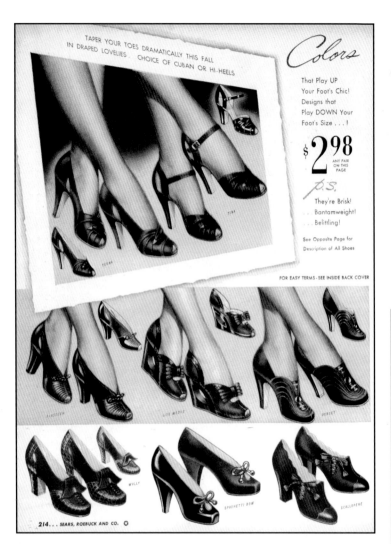

Colors play up your foot's chick, $3. [$35-50] Fall/winter 1940

Choice of the finest styles, bags of Vachelle, $1 each. [$5-15] Fall/winter 1940

Color gives a lift to your life, adds spice to your costume, $2. [$35-45] Fall/winter 1940

Beguiling veiled hats, $1-$1.50. [$15-25] Fall/winter 1940

Turbans certain to charm, $1-$1.60. [$15-25] Fall/winter 1940

Fashion felts, $1.50. [$15-25] Fall/winter 1940

1941 PLAY FASHIONS ANSWER THE
Call to Colors

(G) $1.98 PAIR

$2.00 PAIR

Two Square Deals in Box Toe Comfort

(F) $1.88 PAIR

Wedge style, platform sole, Indian-style fringe, and trim saddle oxford. [$35-45] Spring/summer 1941

You'll Love
"Punch"

Sparkling With Perforations, Its Butterfly Bow Makes Any Foot Look *tiny!*

WIDTHS
A (Very Narrow)
C (Medium)

Destined to be your pet shoe, in blue, white, or black patent, $2. [$30-40] Spring/summer 1941

Low Dutch wedge, tropic cloth upper, glamorous flatterer, Robin Hood style, and elastic side gore, $1.77-$1.98. [$20-30] Spring/summer 1941

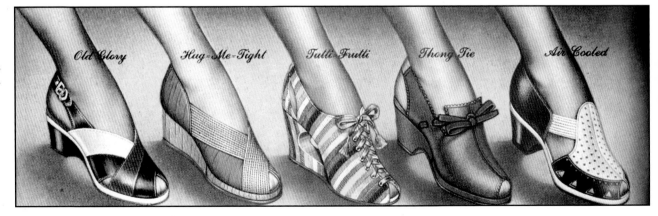

Old Glory *Hug-Me-Tight* *Tutti-Frutti* *Thong Tie* *Air Cooled*

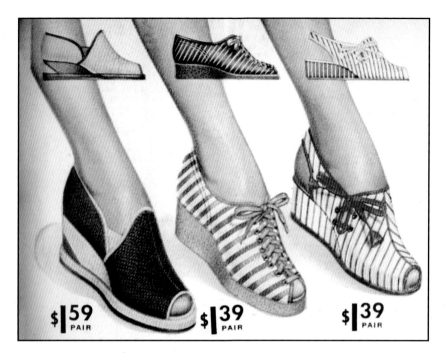

Hopsacking upper, frosty stripes, and cotton pique. [$15-25] Spring/summer 1941

Sun soakers: Tricky ghillie tie, soft cotton suede trim, side lace, and be patriotic right down to your toes. [$20-30] Spring/summer 1941

Elastic gores sculpt feet, wall toe for wiggle room, and smart window wedges, $1.77 each. [$25-35] Spring/summer 1941

Winged bows in flight formation, member of the spectator family, and luxurious young pump, $3 each. [$30-40] Spring/summer 1941

Felt and braid "Kerrybrooke" hats, $1.59 each. [$15-25] Spring/summer 1941

Cover hat with fancy braid, $2. [$15-25] Spring/summer 1941

Turban and glove set, Scotty and glove set, and flattering turban, $1.29-$1.49.
[$15-25] Spring/summer 1941

Flowering turban, blue or rose, and
contrast flowers in black with rose or blue,
$1.79 each. [$10-20] Spring/summer 1941

Felt or
Straw

Felt or
Braid

Pert bolero or Breton charm, black, navy, or white,
$1.69 each. [$20-30] Spring/summer 1941

Our finest Vita Treds with patented "Walk-on-Air" cushion, $4. [$25-35] Fall/winter 1941-42

Woven vamp to wear with slacks, $2, and dress shoe styling, $1. [$20-30] Fall/winter 1941-42

Alligator (grained) matched with suede: fall's number one fashion combination in dressy and tailored styles, $3. [$40-50] Fall/winter 1941-42

84

Turbans to flatter every face, $1.59. [$15-25] Fall/winter 1941-42

Fan front turban, $2. [$15-25] Fall/winter 1941-42

Fan Front Turban

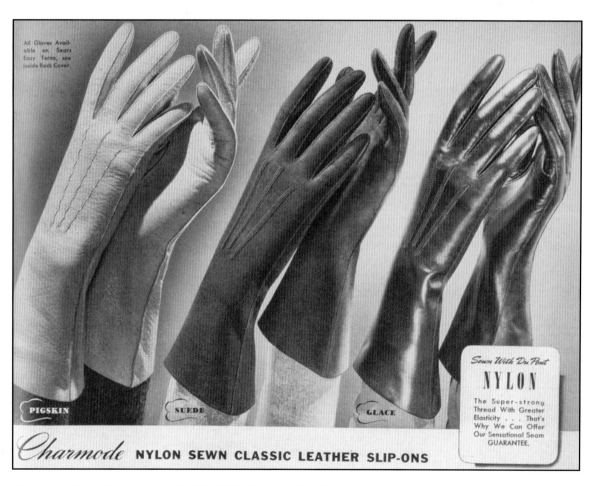

All Gloves Available on Sears Easy Terms, see Inside Back Cover.

PIGSKIN   SUEDE   GLACE

Charmode NYLON SEWN CLASSIC LEATHER SLIP-ONS

Sewn With Du Pont
NYLON
The Super-strong Thread With Greater Elasticity . . . That's Why We Can Offer Our Sensational Seam GUARANTEE.

Sewn classic leather slip-ons, $2. [$5-15] Fall/winter 1941-42

Genuine Mouton Pillbox   Mink Trim

Important "little" hats, moulton pillbox, $2, and mink trim, $3, both in black or brown. [$15-25] Fall/winter 1941-42

Famous designer millinery, Charmode™" large brimmed rayon veiled bonnet, bengaline dressmaker bonnet, wool felt Homberg with eyeline veil, and dressmaker tam with softly shirred brim, $2-3. [$15-25] Fall/winter 1942-43

THE LACER

THE 'COVER HAT'

THE BONNET

THE SEASON'S
3
MOST POPULAR
Casuals

Color numbers refer to Color-Graph Preceding Green Section in Back of Book. Read How to Measure on Page 143

The season's three most popular casuals: the Cover Hat, Bonnet, and Lacer, $2. [$15-25] Fall/winter 1941-42

Low heels in brilliant shine, moc-seam vamp, and knobby alligator, $2.45. [$20-35] Fall/winter 1942-43

Pin-money carefrees in notch-vamp moc and saddle, $2. [$10-20] Fall/winter 1942-43

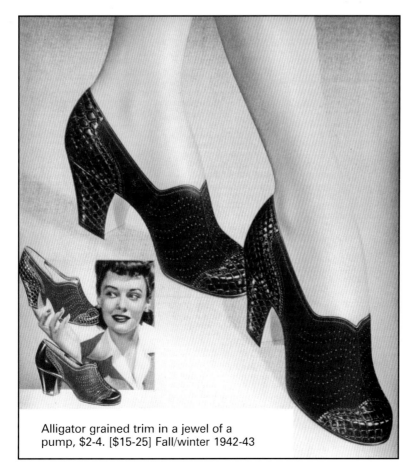

Alligator grained trim in a jewel of a pump, $2-4. [$15-25] Fall/winter 1942-43

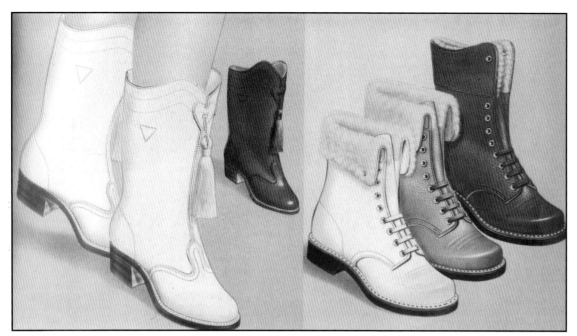

Lead the military fashion parade in majorettes, $4. Snow boot in three colors, with sheep's wool collar, $2.29. [$5-20] Fall/winter 1942-43

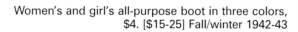

Women's and girl's all-purpose boot in three colors, $4. [$15-25] Fall/winter 1942-43

Teen Girls

Dresses

1940 Fashion Show: staged by the younger crowd. The Dutch Girl, $4. The Basque girl dress with petticoat, $5. The jumper girl skirt and blouse, $3. [$5-15] Fall/winter 1939-40

Newest Fashions: Dutch treat, slim princess, check mates, petticoat ruffle, and 1940 classic. $1.98 each. [$5-15] Fall/winter 1939-40

Fits the Junior Figure of Every Age. [$5-15] Fall/winter 1939-40

Famous $1 cotton dresses: Highland lassie and drum major. [$5-15] Fall/winter 1940

The Junior Jury says "more color." Two-piece crepe dress with gilt embroidery; angel baby long waistline and dancing skirt; campus star softly tailored dress, and hood winker, $3-4. [$5-15] Fall/winter 1940

The Junior Jury says "More Color"

"Hoods are good . . . bright shiny embroidery is exciting.
We like 2-piece dresses . . . We're happy in pastels"

<table>
<tr><td>Ⓓ"Two Timer"
$3.98</td><td>Ⓔ"Angel Baby"
$3.98</td><td>Ⓕ"Campus Star"
$2.98</td><td>Ⓖ"Hood Winker"
$3.98</td></tr>
</table>

Ⓓ"Two Timer"
"Just look at the gilt embroidery-flashing on the front of this two-piece Celanese Rayon Pebble Crepe dress! The jacket is snugly fitted with a Crown zip right up the front! The contrasting colored skirt is divinely flared. My dearest date dress! And no wonder!"
Colors: Aqua Blue top or Pastel Rose top, each with Black skirt. . . .
Juniors' Size Range: 11, 13, 15, 17, 19. *State size and color; Size Scale, Page 38.* Shipping weight, 1 pound 6 ounces.
31 F 8600 . . . .$3.98

Ⓔ"Angel Baby"
"I adore this soft, not too fancy dress. It has the new long waistline, and a dancing skirt! 2 rows of buttons for fun! tie-back sash; Crown zip neck closing and placket. It's made of Tecoko—Spun Rayon and 50% fine Teca Rayon, which makes it look and feel like soft Wool." (Story on Page 50.)
Colors: Misty Rose (as shown), Misty Aqua Blue, or Royal Blue 569.
Juniors' Size Range: 11, 13, 15, 17, 19. *State size and color;* Size Scale, Page 38. Shpg. wt., 1 lb. 6 oz.
31 F 8602 . . . .$3.98

Ⓕ"Campus Star"
"I couldn't resist this softly tailored dress! Just see the neat, bloused top with its pocket-like tabs. The swoopy skirt and set-on belt for smooth waistline— (half each two in front or back). Long sleeves for chic, gilt buttons for glitter! Blissful colors in dull Spun Rayon, 20% fine Teca Rayon (see Page 50).
Colors: Dark Cadet Blue, Scarlet, or Henna Rust 565.
Juniors' Size Range: 11, 13, 15, 17, 19. *State size, color.* Size Scale, Page 38. Shpg. wt., 1 lb. 4 oz.
31 F 8604 . . . .$2.98

Ⓖ"Hood Winker"
Ernestine Cline of Little Rock, Arkansas, sponsors a "Bright with Black" dress—like this—the hooded button-front jacket is Spun Rayon, and 30% fine Teca Rayon, the front-fulled skirt is printed Spun Rayon. Unusual contrast —bright color, tiny checks!
Colors: Scarlet or Kelly Green jacket, each with Black and White Check skirt.
Juniors' Size Range: 11, 13, 15, 17, 19. *State size and color;* see Size Scale on Page 38. Shipping weight, each, 1 lb. 4 oz.
31 F 8606 . . . .$3.98

Use a Colorhelm to learn exciting new color combinations. See Page 47.

Garments on these two pages shipped from our Fashion Headquarters. Send your order to nearest Mail Order House, or, for these garments alone, you may send order directly to New York. You pay postage only from nearest Mail Order House. Color numbers refer to Color-Graph in How to Order section at back of book.

Ⓖ PAGE 35 . . . . DRESSES

"They're beauties" say men who see juniors in them: pin checks, ric-rac rows, huger belt, two-piecer, white flash, and success dress, $1.98 each. [$5-15] Spring/summer 1941

Junior Jury Fashions: casual dress with convertible collar, contrasting belt, trim, and buttons, and beau-catching contrast in dressy style, with princess lines, grosgrain ribbon, $4. [$5-10] Spring/summer 1941

For a junior's busy life: double-featured jacket dress with lace top in navy, black, or cadet blue, $6; pleats-a-plenty in royal blue, rose, or aqua, $5, and coat and dress costume in Kelly green, Copen blue, or Sunset rose, $6. [$5-15] Spring/summer 1941

Fitted and furred with blue-fox dyed lamb, in junior style, $13. [$10-20] Fall/winter 1941-42

Four-way dresses, $2. [$5-15] Fall/winter 1941-42

Dress-up frocks for juniors, $4-7. [$5-15] Fall/winter 1941-42

92

Sears Savers, $2 each. [$5-15] Fall/winter 1941-42

AMY ARDEN   BEA BARTON   CAROL COLE   DOTTIE DEE   EVE EDEN

Greatest values cotton dresses, $2.29 each. [$5-15] Fall/winter 1942-43

Greatest values cotton dresses, $2.29 each. [$5-15] Fall/winter 1942-43

Guaranteed washable cotton dresses, $1.49.
[$5-15] Fall/winter 1942-43

Woven plaids in newest styles, $2-3. [$5-15] Fall/winter 1942-43

Casual Separates and Sportswear

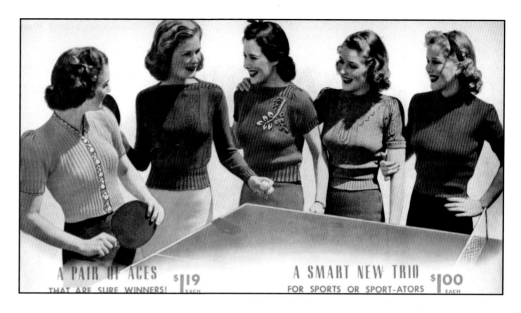

Wool cardigans and pullovers. [$10-20] Fall/winter 1939-40

1940 is a sweater year. [$5-25] Fall/winter 1940

Pullover, $1.39, with matching classic cardigan, $2, or boxy carefree cardigan, $2. [$25-35 sets] Fall/winter 1940

Change-around bib, two-tone or plain shirt and slacks, three-piece stripes with plain includes matching turban, overall set, and trim-fitting overall, $1.30-2. [$15-25] Spring/summer 1941

PRETTIEST, THRIFTIEST PLAY PALS UNDER THE SUN
Carefree Clothes FOR FROLIC AND FUN

Classic $1.39 Pullover

Junior Jury Playmates, $2. [$5-15] Spring/summer 1941-42

Now Low Price on a Winner!
$1.98
Value $2.98
THE FAMOUS CALIFORNIA
Matletex
Play Dress with Panties Attached

Sears 4-Star Feature Because:
★ Famous proven-success fashion . . . a favorite

Junior Jury Playmates
Colors gay as sunshine . . . Action-free cut and a fine figure-fit

An ideal school wardrobe of thrifty good mixers, $1.59-$3.49. [$5-15] Fall/winter 1941-42

Junior "Change-arounds," $1-3. [$5-15] Spring/summer 1941-42

Joan Bradley, Jr. Classics pullovers and cardigans, $1-2. [$5-15] Fall/winter 1941-42

Kerrybrooke sweaters, $1. [$5-15] Fall/winter 1941-42

Well dressed school girls love Kerrybrooke Jr. sweaters, $1-2. [$5-15] Fall/winter 1942-43

Beautiful all wool sweaters, $2. [$5-15] Fall/winter 1942-43

Outerwear

Four styles that stand out: Double-breasted with high collar, rust, teal, or grape, $5. Reversible sports coat for zipping to classes or riding the rumble, brown or henna rust, $8. Squared off shoulders make you more dashing, matching ascot scarf keeps you completely warm, navy, rust, or green, $5. Queen of the crowd, black Persian-effect fur fabric collar, black or wine, $10. [$15-25] Fall/winter 1939-40

Matching hat, scarf, and glove sets. [$5-10]
Fall/winter 1939-40

Leather boots with sheepskin cuffs. [$10-25] Fall/winter 1939-40

"Snowonder" suits. [$5-15] Fall/winter 1939-40

Warm coat successes for the young crowd. [$5-15] Fall/
winter 1939-40

Sally's new wool suit, $6, and Peggy's "Butterball" jacket,
$12. [$5-15] Fall/winter 1939-40

Warmth without bulk: two-piece value suit, ski slacks scoop, and streamlined ski pants. [$10-20] Fall/winter 1939-40

The hooded polo coat, $14, and plaid for juniors, $5. [$5-15] Fall/winter 1939-40

The new coat story for Class-Mates 6 to 14. [$5-10] Fall/winter 1939-40

Face-flattering for dress, school, or sports. [$5-15] Fall/winter 1939-40

Pert styles with a
young outlook
take top honors.
[$5-15] Fall/winter
1939-40

White collar coats: gores in a pretty whirl, detailed to
look like a million, and Sears Original Junior Jury Girl,
$6-13. [$5-15] Spring/summer 1941

Youthful Coats in Colors That Sing

The shorty in stop-light red..
A Tweed-toned classic coat..
Gay double-color reversible
and a plaid in tender pastels

Boyish shorty coat, mannish
topcoat, hooded reversible, and
swagger coat in new pastels, $4-7.
[$5-15] Spring/summer 1941

WARM HEADWEAR GOES *Glamorous!*

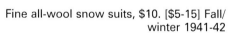

Fine all-wool snow suits, $10. [$5-15] Fall/
winter 1941-42

Snug and warm for dress or play, 35¢-$1.69. [$5-10] Fall/
winter 1941-42

Flemish Bonnet   Snappy Suede Pillbox   Flowered Bonnet

Flemish bonnet, snappy suede pillbox, and flowered bonnet,
$1-2. [$10-20] Fall/winter 1941-42

Beautifully tailored coats for all occasions,
$13. [$5-15] Fall/winter 1942-43

Matching coats for sisters, $9-10. [$5-15] Fall/winter
1942-43

Biggest values in Juniorettes coats, $10-14. [$5-15] Fall/winter 1942-43

Juniorettes Snowonder

24-ox. All-purpose snow pants, $3-4. [$5-15] Fall/winter 1942-43

With button-in quilted lining $15.98

$13⁹⁸ Each **Our biggest values in Coats for sizes 10 to 16**
Each made of good-looking, long-life fabrics and finished with fine tailoring
See descriptions on opposite page

A B C

$9⁹⁸ Each **Our biggest values in Coats for sizes 6 to 10**
Each made with good-looking, long-life fabrics and finished with fine tailoring
See descriptions on opposite page

D E F G

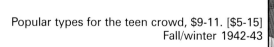

Popular types for the teen crowd, $9-11. [$5-15] Fall/winter 1942-43

A B C D

Men's Fashions

Suits and Dress Wear

Left: Clothes don't make the man, but they help a lot: Worsted wool fabric, double breasted or regular vest, dark blue, dark gray, or green, $16.95. [$5-15] Fall/winter 1939-40

Right: You see it everywhere, this new demand for youth and pep in men's fashions. New three-button drape tweed, brown or green; herringbone worsted wool, pocketed double-breasted, green or blue. $15.95 [$5-15] Fall/winter 1939-40

Swing kings: herringbone cheviot with sporty reversible vest, $15, and virgin wool double-breasted vest, $17. [$5-15] Fall/winter 1939-40

Only $2 Down

Deluxe wool worsteds, expertly tailored. [$5-15] Fall/winter 1939-40

Hollywood styles: New "chesty front" all wool and fancy weave in New drape style, $15 each. [$5-15] Fall/winter 1939-40

Fashion tailored supreme: stripes with over plaid, herringbone silk stripe, and multiple silk stripes, $22.50 each. [$5-15] Fall/winter 1939-40

All wool worsteds and tweeds, $15. [$5-15] Fall/winter 1939-40

Dressy three-button model with silk cluster stripes; semi-drape model with new accentuated chest; sparkling overplaid in long wearing worsted, and a popular model with 100% virgin wool worsted, $18-23. [$5-15] Spring/summer 1941

Handsome well made, low priced bargans, $1.89-2.29. [$5-10] Spring/summer 1941

Virgin Wool serge suits, the nation's greated values. [$5-15] Spring/summer 1941

Smart, stylish summer slacks in cotton, rayon, and worsted wool, $2-5. [$5-15] Spring/summer 1941

Supreme fashion tailored, virgin wool worsted suits, $24.50. [$5-15] Fall/winter 1941-42

Handsome all wool worsteds

Hard finished fabrics in favorite patterns and most popular styles

Handsome all wool worsteds, $20-23. [$5-15] Fall/winter 1942-43

Colorful wool tweed, $18, and wool worsted covert for sports, $24. [$5-15] Fall/winter 1941-42

Favorite fabrics and fashions

Popular patterns are pleasing . . . perfect tailoring assures proper fit

Favorite fabrics and fashions, $20-23.
[$5-15] Fall/winter 1942-43

Spectator sports and business wear suits,
$14-22. [$5-15] Fall/winter 1942-43

114

Good looking styles and patterns

Tailored for easy fitting comfort . . . economically priced

EARL-GLO

All Sears suits are lined with smooth, lustrous genuine Earl-Glo luxurious rayon, guaranteed for the life of garment

Good looking styles and patterns, $14-22.
[$5-15] Fall/winter 1942-43

Choice patterns, all wool suits, $15-20. [$5-15] Fall/winter 1942-43

Service Work Clothes

None Finer Than
Hercules
Sanforized-Shrunk
Coverts

$2.15
OUTFIT PRICE

89¢
Shirt Only

$1.35
Pants Only

Dark Tan

Powder Blue

Forest Green

Over 10% stronger than ordinary coverts. [$15-25] Spring/summer 1941

Drum Major Sanforized-shrunk 8-oz. denim, 97¢. [$50-75] Spring/summer 1941

Slack Suits in Sanforized gabardine, and lustrous shadow stripes for leisure or sports time, green, blue, and tan, $3-4. [$20-30] Spring/summer 1941

Staunton

See Page 320
for How to
Measure

Slack suits in Shantung-effect poplin or cotton/rayon suiting, blue, tan, green, $2-3. [$20-30] Spring/summer 1941

Super Hercules 16-1/2 oz. corduroys, $3. [$35-50] Fall/winter 1941-42

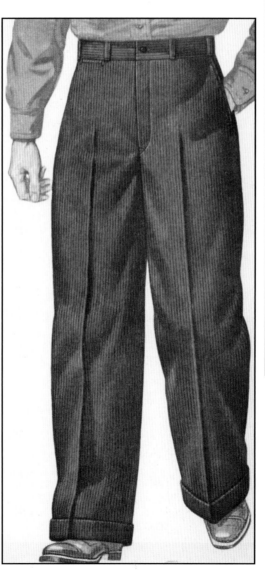

Gabardine and worsted covert slacks, $4-7. [$5-15] Fall/winter 1941-42

Pacemaker Matched Outfits

Matched outfits in sanforized army twills and popular herringbones, $3-5. [$10-20] Fall/winter 1942-43

Neat, strong, and sanforized, $3-7. [$10-20] Fall/winter 1942-43

Bandtops slacks, $1, and overalls, $1.10. [$50-75] Fall/winter 1942-43

Zip fly, reinforced pockets

Heaviest work shirt, $1.15. [$5-10] Fall/winter 1942-43

Bargain leader coveralls, $2-3. [$20-50] Fall/winter 1942-43

Roomy and perfect-fitting
Nation-Alls
OUR OWN TRADE MARK

Look at the figures at the left. Every one has the same size chest, but each has a different crotch-to-shoulder measurement. We made our own special patterns—graduated to give each inseam size the proper "rise" from crotch to shoulder. That means no more tight binding crotches—no more droopy, baggy seats. You can be sure Nation-Alls fit you right, whatever your build. Be sure you give us your exact chest, waist and inseam measurements when ordering.

Fabric weighs 5 oz. per sq. yd.

Khaki

White twill

Hickory stripe

Blue denim

White twill

Hickory stripe

Gray covert

Khaki twill

Action back

119

Casual Sportswear

America's No. 1 hunting outfit, water repellent
wool coat, breeches, and cap. [$5-15 each]
Fall/winter 1939-40

Zip pocket, capeskin front, $3, all wool, $2, or soft napped, $3. [$10-20] Fall/winter 1939-40

ALL WOOL TWIN SETS
YOU CAN AFFORD THE BEST! FOR EASY
TERMS SEE INSIDE OF BACK COVER . .

PULLOVER
SWEATERS

$198 EACH

Wool twin sets, $2-4. [$10-20] Fall/
winter 1939-40

Zip-front sweaters, $2-5. [$10-20] Fall/
winter 1939-40

Sports shirts in a wide choice of colors, 79¢-$2. [$5-15] Spring/summer 1941

Virgin wool worsted in overplaid
pattern, $3, and tailored worsted, $4.
[$5-15] Fall/winter 1941-42

Sportswear, $13-18 for ensembles. [$5-15] Fall/winter 1941-42

Fine trousers of all-wool corded gabardine and wool worsted, $7-8. [$5-15] Fall/winter 1942-43

Chalk stripes on sturdy, hard finished fabric, and fine Shetland-type fabric in smooth herringbone weave, $4.50-$5. [$5-15] Fall/winter 1942-43

New "baby shaker" soft wool pullovers, $2-3. [$5-15] Fall/winter 1942-43

Warm winter Sports Shirts

Wool/rayon gabardine, $4, and all wool raglan sleeves, $5. [$5-15] Fall/winter 1942-43

All wool "twin sets, $4-5. [$25-35] Fall/winter 1942-43

Gabardine shirts with two-way collars, $2-3. [$5-15] Fall/winter 1942-43

All wool shirts in big, bold buffalo checks, $4-6. [$5-15]
Fall/winter 1942-43

Underwear and Sleepwear

Good royalton cotton, Imperial crest, soft knit jersey top, and cotton broadcloth, 79¢-$1.59. [$5-15] Fall/winter 1939-40

Equal to 39¢ in most stores, 29¢, or 4 for $1.12. [$2-5] Fall/winter 1939-40

Fuzzy Wuzzys, America's No. 1 slipper sensation puts you "two feet deep" in comfort, $2, kitskin handturns, $2. [$5-10] Fall/winter 1941-42

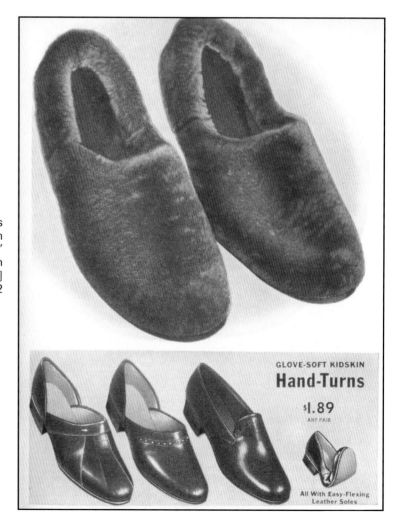

GLOVE-SOFT KIDSKIN
Hand-Turns
$1.89
ANY PAIR

All With Easy-Flexing Leather Soles

All with easy-flexing leather soles

Black or Brown

F

G Choice of Burgundy Black or Brown

H Two-tone... Burgundy with Blue

Genuine kidskin slippers, $2.39. [$10-20] Fall/winter 1942-43

Brocaded rayon Wrap model

$4.98 Each)

Rayon jacquard Full rayon Lining

$8.35 Each

Brocaded rayon wrap, $5, and jacquard with full rayon lining, $8.35. [$10-20] Fall/winter 1942-43

Extra heavyweight Beacon blanket cloth robe, $6.50. [$30-50] Fall/winter 1942-43

127

Comfortable knit pajamas, $2. [$5-10] Fall/winter 1942-43

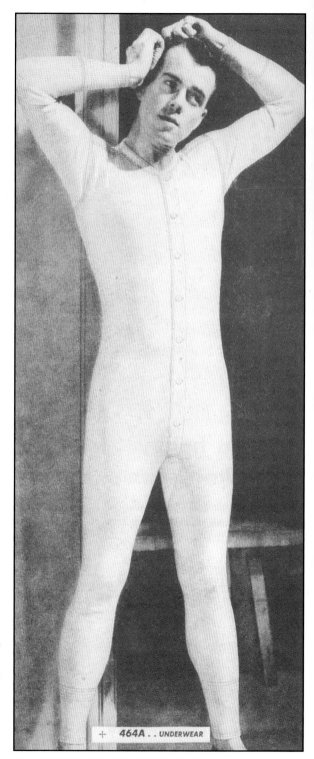

Best union suit in wool and wool/
cotton blends, $3-$6.50. [$5-10]
Fall/winter 1942-43

+ 464A . . UNDERWEAR

Outerwear

Our finest topcoats: dressy double-vested wool, $17, and genuine camel's hair and wool, $20. [$10-20] Fall/winter 1939-40

$16.50

$17.45

See Opposite Page for Descriptions of Coats Shown Above and Below

$13.85

$14.45

Fashion tailored overcoats, $20. [$10-20] Fall/winter 1939-40

All-wool topcoats for youth and younger fellows, too. [$10-20] Fall/winter 1939-40

Our FINEST POLO STYLE TOPCOAT.. All Wool and Mohair Beautifully Tailored

ALL WOOL TOPCOATS

Styled for Youth and Older Fellows, Too ● Warm, Serviceable—Can Be Worn the Year 'round ● Low Priced

Swagger coats keep you warm
and dry: waterproof coat in
dapper herringbone, reversible
all-weather top coat, and "DeLuxe
Buckskein," $3-5. [$15-25]
Spring/summer 1941

Stay dry, dressy, in swagger styles, $8. [$10-20]
Fall/winter 1941-42

Gabardine bound brim, two-way
snap brim, and plain edge snap brim.
[$5-15] Fall/winter 1941-42

Warmly lined wool mackinaw,
$6. [$10-20] Fall/winter 1941-42

Lined wool and mohair
Buckskein mackinaw, $7.45.
[$10-20] Fall/winter 1941-42

Richly colored popular plaid, $10. [$5-15]
Fall/winter 1941-42

Sport style in all virgin wool, two-tone coat $10. [$5-15] Fall/winter 1941-42

Our most popular jacket with stitched half belt, in capeskin or suede, $9.50. [$45-55] Fall/winter 1942-43

Removable lined Parka hood keeps entire head warm

Coat and parka hood lined with alpaca pile, $13. [$10-20] Fall/winter 1942-43

132

Big, comfortable Coat

Big comfortable coat, double-breasted, $12. [$5-15] Fall/winter 1942-43

Bengora overcoats in youthful fly-front models and smart double-breasted model, $22.45. [$5-15] Fall/winter 1942-43

Felt hats with 2-1/2-, 2-5/8-, and 2-1/4-inch brims, $2.14. [$5-15]
Fall/winter 1942-43

Quality topcoats of wool, double-
or single-breasted, $17-19. [$5-
15] Fall/winter 1942-43

Shoes

D (Medium Wide)
EEE (Triple Wide)
in These Three Shoes

Custom Toes . . . Dressy and Comfortable

$2.89 Briargates are worth more: you get $4 styling, $4 leathers, $4 wear, $4 comfort. [$15-25] Spring/summer 1941

Genuine Calfskin

Genuine Calfskin

← WASHABLE! This Smooth Leather Can be Cleaned Quickly With Soap and Water

Neat French toes: American favorites year after year, $3.35. [$15-25] Spring/summer 1941

Styled the American way ... full wing tips that strut with style, $3. [$20-30] Spring/summer 1941

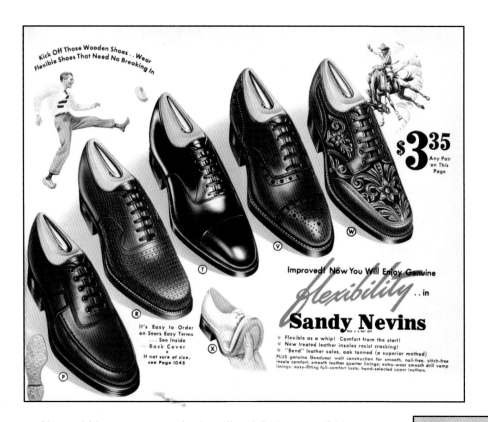

New cobble-sewn moccasin, "ventilateds", dressy calfskin uppers, husky military type brogue, the buckaroo with embossed hints of Western saddles, $3.35. [$15-30] Spring/ summer 1941

Husky, hefty, handsome sports styles, $3.19. [$20-35] Spring/ summer 1941

Pre-flexed at the factory: leather sole brogue and crepe rubber sole "Rodeo," $3. [$20-30] Fall/winter 1941-42

Ready to follow a man's foot in action: air pilot, saddle stitched, cobble-sewn "Mac," Western thriller, and Genuine calfskin, $3.55. [$20-30] Fall/winter 1941-42

$365
Any pair of Briargates on these two pages

See facing page for complete descriptions of all these Shoes

☐ PAGE 261 .... MEN'S SHOES

Easy on your feet, easy on your pocketbook. [$20-30] Fall/winter 1942-43

Pegged shanks with calfskin uppers, $5. [$20-30] Fall/winter 1942-43

Burgundy brown genuine calfskin

Teen Boys

Dress Wear

Wool suits: one-button model, two-way vest, athletic style, and swing kings, $12-17. [$5-15] Fall/winter 1939-40

Wool suits, $5-12. [$5-15] Fall/winter 1939-40

Boys! Fine all wool fabrics in dressy double breasteds. [$5-15] Fall/winter 1939-40

Tailored sports clothes: stylish overplaid, wool worsted gabardine, Navy cheviot, coat and slacks, and all-wool outfit. [$5-15] Spring/summer 1941

The College Shop: A "twosome" in Shetland type tweed, $15; herringbones go to "thick yarns," $13, and Donegal type tweed three-button model, $15. [$5-15] Fall/winter 1939-40

SEARS COLLEGE SHOP

Smart styles for campus
leaders, $11-15. [$5-15]
Spring/summer 1941

NEWEST SPORTS COATS AND SLACKS

Newest sports coats and slacks, $3-13. [$5-15]
Fall/winter 1941-42

Smart sports ensemble · All wool suiting · Sturdy, hard finish

Smart, expertly tailored suits, $10-13. [$5-15] Fall/winter 1942-43

Casual

Patterned corduroys in campus styles, $3. [$20-35] Fall/winter 1939-40

The Style hit of the season: "Leisure" coat plus slacks, $4. [$5-15] Spring/summer 1941

Wool pants, $3. [$5-15] Fall/winter 1939-40

Slack Suits .. for Young All-Americans!

Sports shirts for boys, 49¢-79¢ [$5-10] Spring/summer 1941

Sports Shirts for Boys
Cool Fabrics .. a World of Style

Wear 'em In or Out of Trousers

Husky all wool flannels in Buffalo checks … favored by outdoor men for years, $3. [$5-15] Fall/winter 1941-42

Slack Suits, Sanforized-shrunk to keep perfect fit, $2-3.[$10-20] Spring/summer 1941

The finest coat style sweater we've ever offered – inside shoulder yoke, whipstitch pockets, double-fabric elbows, $3. [$5-10] Fall/winter 1942-43

Outdoor shirts in cotton flannels, 77¢-$1.07. [$5-10] Fall/winter 1942-43

Outerwear

Both these Jackets fully lined with lustrous Earl-Glo Rayon

Capeskin leather jackets for boys 8-18, $8-10. [$30-50] Fall/winter 1942-43

Fashion favorite fingertip coat in genuine "Velofleece" of all wool face and invisible, knit cotton back, $12. [$5-15] Fall/winter 1942-43

Warm and practical Reversibles

Warm cotton flannel lining throughout

Warm reversibles gabardine coat style, zip-front jacket, $5. Warm, fur-like pile lining, $4.59. [$10-20] Fall/winter 1942-43

DeLuxe aviator-style leather combination jacket, $5.25. [$20-30] Fall/winter 1942-43

Sleepwear

Short sleeve
ankle length style

Short sleeve
knee length style

Long sleeve,
ankle length style

PAGE 373

Genuine Beacon blanket robe, $4; heavy-weight napped cotton plaid, $3. [$25-35; 5-10] Fall/winter 1942-43

Cotton union suits, 67¢-85¢ [$5-10] Fall/winter 1942-43

Children

Our best bib outfit; swanky style, popular suspender suit, and gay sailor suit. [$5-15] Fall/winter 1939-40

Junior breeches, fine for school! [$2-5] Fall/winter 1939-40

Fool old man winter, with lined outdoor suits, blue, brown, green: wool $6, half-wool $3. [$10-20] Fall/winter 1939-40

Winter's lots of fun. [$5-15] Fall/winter 1939-40

Finely woven, long wearing suitings. [$5-15] Fall/winter 1939-40

THEY'RE PRACTICAL!
Each Style Warmly Lined End to End
Genuine Sheepskin
69¢ Ea.
Streamlined style and warmth combined. Select quality sheepskin leather with soft cotton lining. Goggles can be worn up, down or off completely. Perforated ear flaps. Strap has sliding adjustable buckle which fastens under chin.
Sizes: 6⅜ to 7⅛. State size. Shipping weight, each, 11 ounces.
93 D 4905—Black
93 D 4906—Brown
Sporty Looking
39¢ Ea.
Genuine DuPont fabricoid . . . resembles leather. Comfortably pliable, yet made to give good service. Warm cotton lining, snap-fastened goggles. Adjustable chin strap with sliding buckle for better fit. Perforated eyelets over ears.
Sizes: 6⅜ to 7⅛. State size. Shipping weight, each, 9 ounces.
93 D 4920—Black
93 D 4921—Brown
Select Horsehide
$1.19 Each
It's Sears best helmet . . . just as outstanding in style as it is in quality! Made of long-wearing horsehide . . . with a new high style note added by the bright laskin lamb trim. Can be worn up, or with the furry laskin lamb flaps right against the face. Warm cotton flannel lining. Strap has sliding adjustable buckle which fastens under chin.
Colors: Black with Red Trim, or Brown with Green Trim.
Sizes: 6⅜ to 7⅛. Shipping weight, each, 8 ounces.
93 D 4914—State size, color.
HOW TO MEASURE
State your boy's correct hat or cap size, if you know it. If not, place a tape measure (or strip of paper which can be measured afterward) around head as shown. Then refer to chart at right and order size corresponding to his measurement.
If Head Measure Is / Order Size
19 to 19¼ 6⅛
19⅜ to 19⅝ 6¼
19¾ to 20 6⅜
20⅛ to 20⅜ 6½
20½ to 20¾ 6⅝
20⅞ to 21⅛ 6¾
21¼ to 21½ 6⅞
21⅝ to 21⅞ 7
22 to 22¼ 7⅛
22⅜ to 22⅝ 7¼

They're practical, genuine sheepskin, sporty looking. [$5-15] Fall/winter 1939-40

Three-piece tweed suit, classy four-piece suit, zip pocket suit, and 3-piece sailor suit, $1-$1.69. [$5-15] Fall/winter 1941-42

Baby Billy knows how to keep snug, he wears a Bird cloth carriage suit, $4. [$5-15] Fall/winter 1939-40

Heavyweight, rib knit cotton union suits, 45¢-55¢. [$2-5] Fall/winter 1939-40

Deeply Napped Flannelette Pajamas for Boys 6 to 18

Elastic Inserts in Waist for Comfort
SANFORIZED-SHRUNK
For Lasting Fit

Pajamas, 69¢-$1.27. [$2-5] Fall/winter 1939-40

THE NEW BUTCHER-BOY TEAM-MATES
Jitter-Jamas
NOW—FOR MOTHER AND DAUGHTER
- Gripper Fasteners on the Adjustable Waist Trousers
- Double Needle Seams
- Full Comfortable Cut in Boxy Butcher-Boy Style
- Fine Washfast Percale

Women's Sizes $119 Ea.

Girls' Sizes 98¢ Ea.

Jitter-Jamas, now for mother and daugher. [$5-10]
Spring/summer 1941

Sanforized Slack Suits

For Juniors 4 to 10

All These Slack Suits are Tailored With
Elastic Waist Band Inserts . . to Assure a
Snug Comfortable Fit . . Won't Bind

Leisure style coat, Nautical style, and Zip-pocket
style slack suits, $1.50-$2.50. [$5-15] Spring/summer
1941

Sportswear for Sally's
7 to 14'ers, 59¢-$1.98.
[$5-15] Spring/
summer 1941

Slack suits with striped slacks, blue cotton
suiting, and slub poplin. [$5-15] Spring/
summer 1941

Spring values for growing girls, lovely, long-wearing dresses and sportswear, $1 each. [$5-15] Spring/summer 1941

Joan Bradley, Jr. classics: pullover, $1.29; classic cardigan popular hip length, $1.79, and long boxy cardigan … America's sweater sweetheart, $1.79. [$10-20] Fall/winter 1941-42

An ideal school wardrobe of thrifty good mixers, $1.59-$3.49. [$5-10] Fall/winter 1941-42

Bib-top ski pants, water-resistant outdoor suit, and sturdy outdoor suit, $3 each. [$5-15] Fall/winter 1941-42

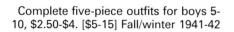

Snowwonder suits for juniorettes, $8-10. [$5-15]
Fall/winter 1941-42

[$] Fall/winter 1941-42

Complete five-piece outfits for boys 5-
10, $2.50-$4. [$5-15] Fall/winter 1941-42

Military styles for boys 3-14, $3-4.50. [$20-35] Fall/winter 1942-43

Honeysuckles™ for 3 to 6-1/2's, $1. [$5-15] Fall/winter 1942-43

Anne

Polly

Bonnie

Doris

Sally

Rough 'n' ready playclothes for 1-4's, $1. [$5-15] Fall/winter 1942-43

Shortie suits, $1-$3.50.
[$5-10] Fall/winter 1942-
43

Two-piece undies for children 2 to 8, 45¢. [$5-10] Fall/
winter 1942-43

Longie suits for
dress or play,
$2.50-$3. [$5-10]
Fall/winter 1942-
43

Navy blue cheviot   With knit shirt   Corduroy Longies with Shirts

Two-piece overcoat sets with zip leggings, $6-9. [$5-10] Fall/winter 1942-43

Warm outdoor suits, $7-9. [$5-10] Fall/winter 1942-43